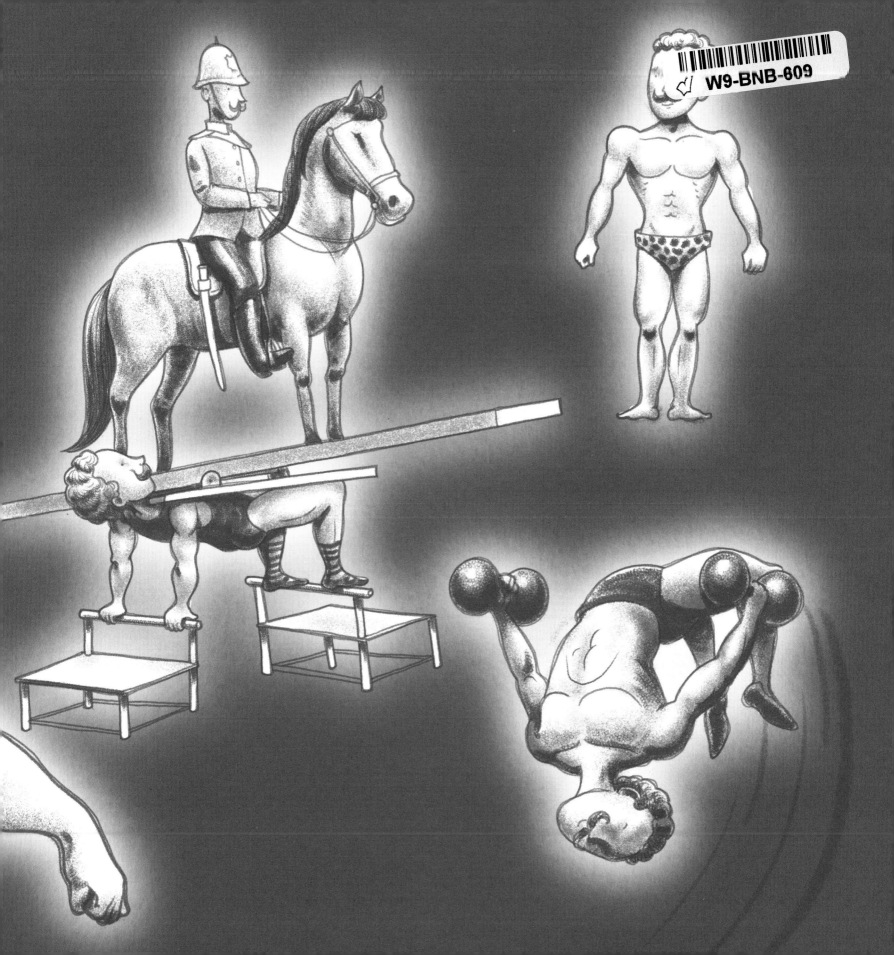

STRONG AS SANDOW

How Eugen Sandow Became the Strongest Man on Earth

Don Tate

ⁱ⌂ⁱ Charlesbridge

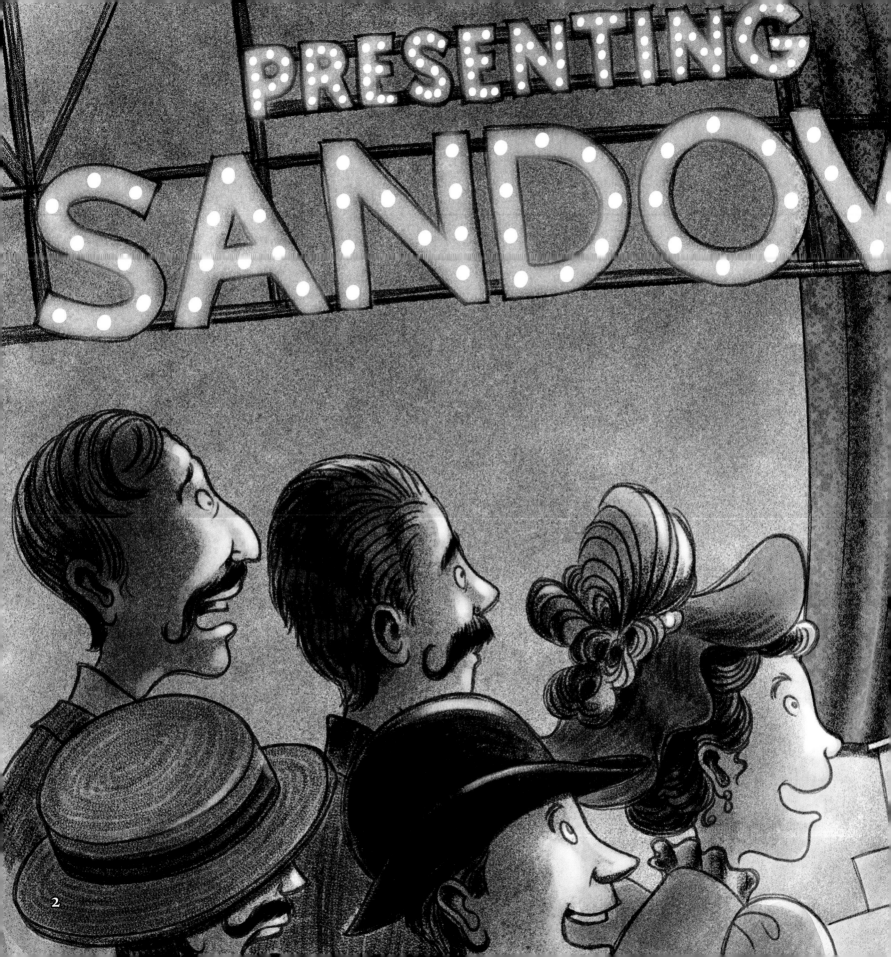

In his day Eugen Sandow was known as "the Strongest Man on Earth." He could break metal chains by expanding his broad chest. He could hoist a grand piano over his head.

He boasted that he once wrestled a five-hundred-pound lion.

No doubt Eugen Sandow was the strongest of all strongmen. But he wasn't always strong.

The Delicate Days

Königsberg, Prussia, 1867–1885?

His birth name was Friedrich Wilhelm Müller. As a boy, he loved athletics. But playing sports required a strong, healthy body. Friedrich's arms were skinny, and his legs were as frail as twigs. He looked downright feeble. Often, he was too sick to play.

But Friedrich survived. His spirit was strong. He played sports, and he excelled in school. As a reward for his high honors, his father took him on a trip to Italy. They visited the famous art galleries of Rome.

Friedrich was awestruck by the statues of ancient athletes. Their muscles looked so powerful. If only he could look like a Roman gladiator!

"How is it that these men were so strong, Father?" Friedrich asked.

"The heroes of old," his father said, "were ever active, ever exercising their bodies."

7

Exercise—that was it! To make his body stronger, Friedrich would need to push himself even harder. When he returned home, he ran longer and jumped higher. He exercised like never before.

But his ten-year-old body wasn't ready to bloom just yet.
To Friedrich's despair, it remained weak and puny.

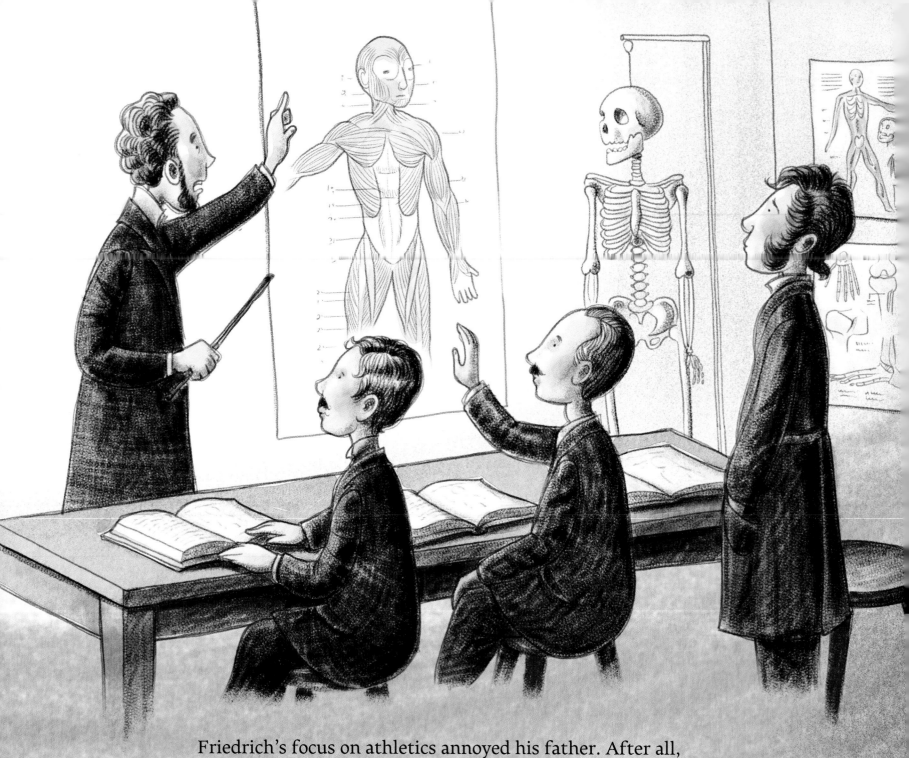

Friedrich's focus on athletics annoyed his father. After all,
exercise might be good for the body, but what about the mind?
He wanted his son to devote more time to finding a career. He sent
Friedrich, now in his late teens, away to study at a university.

At school Friedrich learned about anatomy—bones, muscles,
the human form—

but he longed to do something more
physically active.

Strong and Stronger
Prussia to Belgium, 1885?–1887

One day a traveling circus rolled into town. Friedrich snuck away from school to watch. He was starstruck by the performers— tumblers, wrestlers, acrobats, strongmen. The lure was simply too much to resist. Friedrich left the university and joined the circus. He became an acrobat.

Life as an acrobat was physically demanding. Friedrich tumbled and bent and balanced. He flipped and flopped and stood on his hands. Soon he began to notice a change in his body: his muscles were getting bigger and stronger.

But the circus turned out to be a ragtag operation. It ran out of money, and Friedrich lost the job he so adored.

To support himself, Friedrich found work as a model for art students. His burly, ever-growing physique was the perfect reference for their paintings and sculptures. Through their art, Friedrich became the gladiator he had dreamed of being as a child.

15

One of the artists introduced Friedrich to Professor Attila, a professional strongman. The Professor gave Friedrich a job at his gym and offered to teach him bodybuilding.

"Attend to my instructions," the Professor said, "and I shall be able to make you the strongest man in the world."

The Professor made Friedrich lift heavier weights. The metal barbells were so heavy, Friedrich's muscles quivered. But he didn't complain. The heavier the weights, the bigger his muscles grew.

Friedrich's knowledge about the strongman business grew, too. He learned about showmanship, costumes, and stage presence.

By the time he was twenty years old, Friedrich was a bona fide professional strongman. He even changed his name. Friedrich Müller would be known forever after as Eugen Sandow.

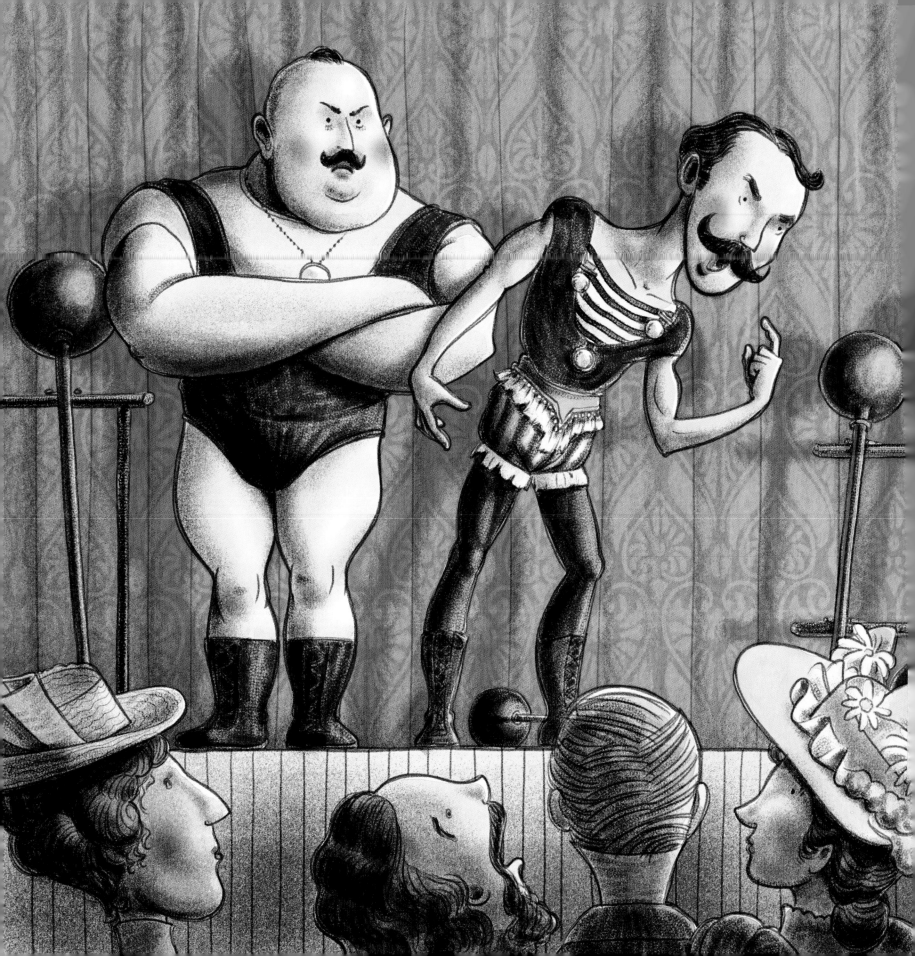

The Big Challenge

London, 1889

Sampson and Cyclops were the greatest professional strongmen of their time. They were brawny. They were brutes. They were loudmouthed, muscle-bound lunks! Sampson and Cyclops lifted horses and elephants as though they were as light as feathers.

Each night after their act in London, they roared out a challenge to the audience: they dared anyone to try to defeat them in a competition of strength. But who would accept such a foolish challenge?

Eugen Sandow, that's who.

Eugen jumped onstage. Dressed in a fine suit, he sauntered along confidently—until he tripped over a barbell and almost fell on his face. Everyone laughed—Sampson and Cyclops hardest of all.

But Eugen had a plan. With one swoop of his powerful arm, he ripped off his suit, all at once. The audience gasped at the sight of his mighty muscles.

The competition began. Sampson and Cyclops jerked pound after pound of incredibly heavy weights above their heads. But each time, Eugen effortlessly met their challenge. Sometimes he lifted more. Sampson raged. Cyclops fumed. At last Eugen was declared the winner.

23

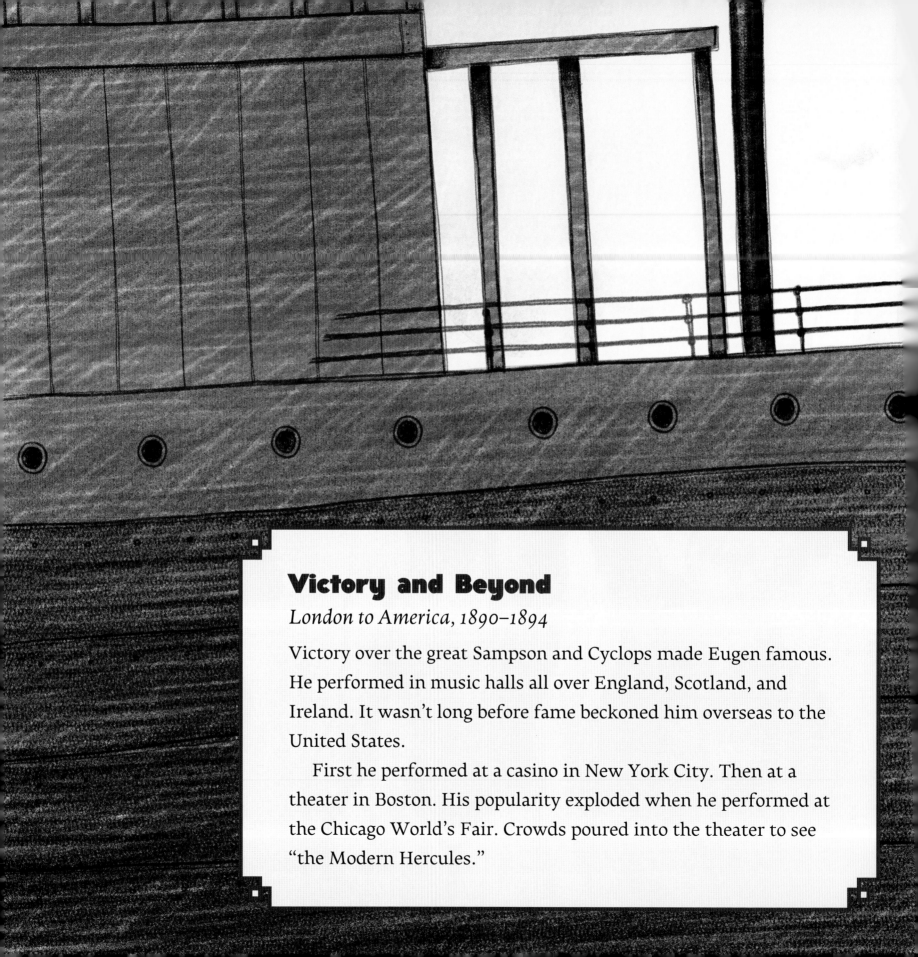

Victory and Beyond

London to America, 1890–1894

Victory over the great Sampson and Cyclops made Eugen famous.
He performed in music halls all over England, Scotland, and
Ireland. It wasn't long before fame beckoned him overseas to the
United States.

First he performed at a casino in New York City. Then at a
theater in Boston. His popularity exploded when he performed at
the Chicago World's Fair. Crowds poured into the theater to see
"the Modern Hercules."

When the curtain rose, Eugen appeared onstage. He was dusted head-to-toe with white powder, which made him look like a living, breathing marble statue. When he lifted a heavy barbell over his head, some people in the audience gasped. Others fainted.

Truth be told, though, no one really cared about how much weight Eugen could lift. They were in awe of his physique. His chiseled muscles were things of beauty, like fine works of art.

After the show in Chicago, Eugen became one of the most famous stars in America.

As Eugen went on to tell it, his greatest moment happened one evening in San Francisco. "The Event of the Century" packed hordes of spectators into a huge, circus-like tent. Inside, a massive lion roared and people shrieked. But Eugen was all confidence and smiles.

When Eugen entered the cage and flexed his hefty muscles,
the king of the beasts cowered down, tame as a kitty. Eugen
scooped up the lion and paraded him around the stage.

The lion wore mittens, and some people thought he looked
drugged. Was it all a trick? A showman's illusion? Eugen Sandow
would never let on.

The so-called fight lasted just a few minutes, and the
strongman was declared the winner.

Home

America to London, 1898–1901

Eugen continued to travel. But over time the grueling schedule proved too much even for him. He became tired and sickly. He lost weight. His once powerful muscles seemed to fade away. His body needed rest, and so did his mind.

Eugen said good-bye to America and returned home to Britain.

For months Eugen rested. While his body recovered, his brain searched for ways to continue his career. He opened a gym. He published books and magazines promoting bodybuilding and nutritious eating. He designed his own equipment and techniques for strengthening muscles.

31

In 1901 Eugen launched the Great Competition—the first organized bodybuilding contest. Strongmen traveled from all over the country to compete at the Royal Albert Hall in London.

But Eugen wasn't interested in rewarding only big, muscular physiques. He considered a man's overall health and physical development, too.

First the men performed athletic displays—wrestling, gymnastics, even fencing. Then, after several rounds of posing, a winner was chosen. He received a cash prize and a gold-plated statue of none other than Eugen Sandow himself.

On the night of the Great Competition, Eugen Sandow performed, too. He must have flexed a smile as broad as his biceps. After all, the once-frail child was now known as "the Strongest Man on Earth." And it seemed that every man on earth—and every woman and child, too—was now devoting more attention to their own health. Everyone wanted to become "as strong as Sandow."

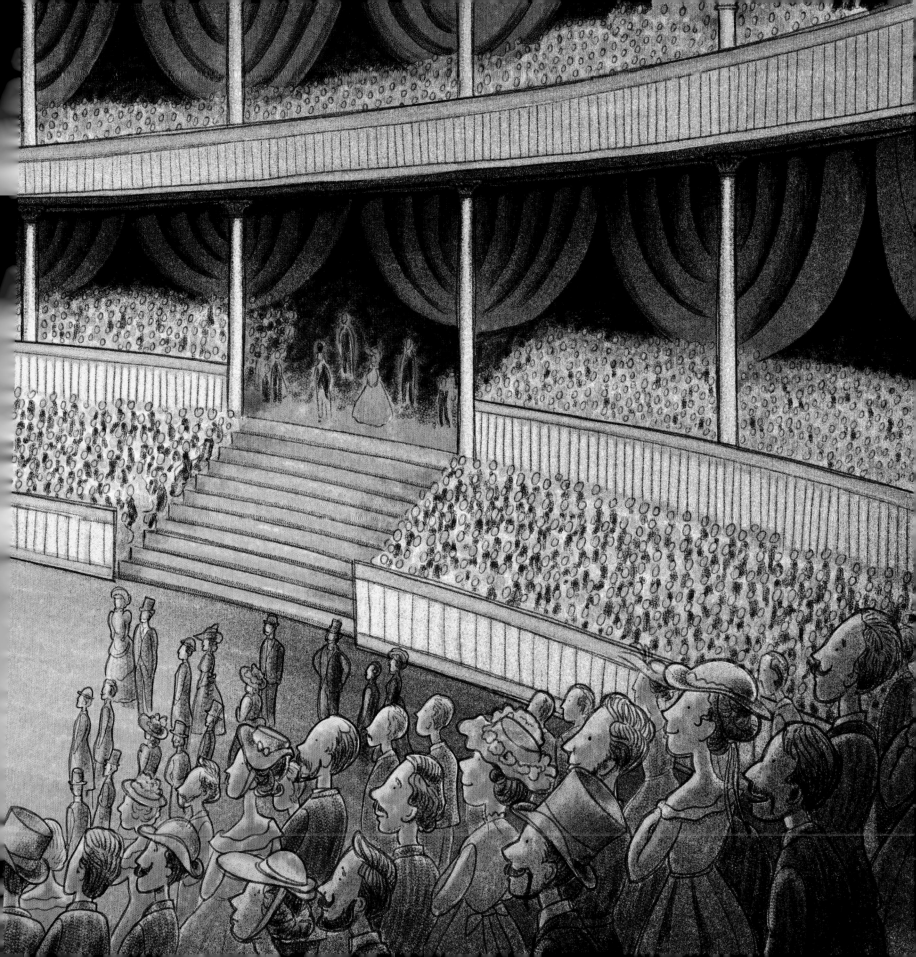

Afterword

David Beckham, LeBron James, and Justin Bieber are modern-day male superstars. During the Victorian era (1837–1901), Eugen Sandow was that star. From England to the United States and beyond, people flocked to see the strongman flex his muscles.

Deemed "the most perfect male specimen alive" by doctors of his time, Sandow was often photographed in the buff, wearing only a fig leaf and high-laced sandals. It was an image that harkened back to the Greek and Roman statues he had so admired as a child. Sandow even measured the proportions of those statues in order to develop his own body to more closely resemble them.

But while Sandow was fixated on looks, he was also passionate about helping others to develop healthier minds and bodies. For children, he advocated a national physical-fitness program in schools. For men, women, and children throughout England, he established schools of physical culture. For everyone around the world, he produced home exercise equipment and dietary supplements. His book *Strength and How to Obtain It* became a best-seller, and his magazine, *Sandow's Magazine of Physical Culture*, was a forerunner to publications such as *Flex* and *Men's Health*.

Sandow's exercises and diet regimens are still in use today, as is the muscled statuette that bears his name: the Sandow. For years, bodybuilding's ultimate prize was a sculpture of a nude, fig-leaf-adorned Sandow clutching a barbell. The original was awarded at the 1901 Great Competition. Today the statuette is the top prize in the Mr. Olympia bodybuilding competition. (For better or for worse, the statuette was recently updated: the Sandow is now beefier, and he's lost the fig leaf in favor of posing trunks.)

In his lifetime Sandow was filmed by no other than Thomas Edison, and a plaster cast of his body was made by the Natural History Museum in London. His followers included celebrities such as Sherlock Holmes creator Arthur Conan Doyle and famed writer James Joyce. He even became the personal fitness instructor to King George V.

Eugen Sandow died in 1925 at the age of 58.

Life Is Movement!

Eugen Sandow believed it was important for everyone, especially kids, to stay physically active—to move! Here are some exercises that you can try at home. With each exercise, be sure to keep your back straight and your belly button tucked in—this will protect your back from injury. Try to repeat each exercise ten times. And don't forget to stretch first!

Push-ups

Balance on your hands and toes, keeping your back straight. Bend your elbows and lower yourself almost to the floor. Pause for a second, then push back up, straightening your arms. Focus on squeezing your chest muscles. Inhale as you go down; exhale as you push up.

Chair squats

Stand a few inches in front of a chair, with your feet apart and your toes facing forward. With your weight on your heels, bend your knees until you are in a sitting position—but don't sit down! Pause for a second, then return to the starting position. Inhale as you lower; exhale as you rise.

Calf raises

Rest one hand on a wall for balance, with your other hand hanging at your side. Rise up onto the balls of your feet. Hold for a second, squeezing your calf muscles, then lower to where you started. Exhale as you rise; inhale as you lower.

Arm raises

If you have a pair of light dumbbells, great. If not, use two water bottles or cans of soup. Stand with your feet apart and your knees slightly bent. Holding a weight in each hand, begin with your arms at your side. Slowly raise your arms until they are in line with your shoulders, palms facing the floor. Hold for a second, and return to where you started. Exhale as you raise your arms; inhale as you lower them.

Author's Note

Don Tate, Upper Midwest Natural Bodybuilding Championships, 1998.

As a kid, I was skinny. Recognizing my anxiety about it, my dad bought me a bench press and a copy of *The Bodybuilder's Nutrition Book*. It featured nutrition information, along with photos of famous bodybuilders like Arnold Schwarzenegger and Lou Ferrigno. I was in awe of their superhero-like physiques. I dreamed of someday having powerful muscles like them.

Years later my younger brother, Brian, got involved in bodybuilding and won a statewide contest. I wondered if I could bulk up and compete, too. At age 32 I began my bodybuilding journey, training with my brother. We lifted weights, attended aerobics classes, practiced compulsory poses.

Two years later I entered my first bodybuilding contest. I was terrified. I sweated a little (something you're not supposed to do). I was having one of the best nights of my life . . . until I lost. I didn't even place. I was devastated, but I didn't give up. I continued to lift weights. I traded candy and sugary drinks for green beans, yams, and chicken breasts. And I perfected my poses. When I competed again the next year, I took home first- and second-place trophies.

Natural bodybuilding is drug free—the use of steroids is forbidden. For that reason, there aren't many garbage-truck-size contestants at these shows. I may not have had the massive muscles of a superhero, but I sure felt like I did.

Although I no longer compete in bodybuilding, I've often thought about writing a book for children about it. But how? One day I stumbled upon a picture of Eugen Sandow online. Relating to his childhood desire to beef up, I decided to tell his story.

Writing Sandow's story was challenging. After his death, Sandow's family destroyed his personal belongings. In addition, books and magazine articles about him often contradict one another. It appears Sandow was not only a builder of muscles, but also a manufacturer of his own story. Historians are still unsure about his parentage and early life. They've even questioned the trip he and his father supposedly made to Rome. And don't even get me started on the controversy over the so-called fight with the lion!

My goal for this book was to tell the story as I think Sandow would have wanted it told, fanciful as that might be. Regardless of his true origins (and a few less-than admirable things I learned about him), the story of Eugen Sandow is an important one. His tale of sickly kid turned physical-fitness guru and self-made businessman inspired millions of people. Through his example, Sandow demonstrated to the world how a healthy body is necessary for a healthy mind. His lesson rings true today.

Bibliography

Art of Manliness. "The Art of Manliness Podcast #39: Eugen Sandow, Victorian Strongman, with David Waller." February 2, 2012. Available online at http://www.artofmanliness.com/2012/02/02/the-art-of-manliness-podcast-39-eugen-sandow-victorian-strongman-with-david-waller/.

Barford, Vanessa, and Lucy Townsend. "Eugen Sandow: The Man with the Perfect Body." *BBC News Magazine*, October 19, 2012. Available online at http://www.bbc.com/news/magazine-19977415.

Buck, Joshua Michael. "The Development of the Performances of Strongmen in American Vaudeville Between 1881 and 1932." Unpublished thesis, University of Maryland at College Park, 1999. Available online at http://joshuabuck.com/about-josh/files/thesis.pdf.

Budd, Michael Anton. *The Sculpture Machine: Physical Culture and Body Politics in the Age of Empire*. New York: New York University Press, 1997.

Chapman, David L. *Sandow the Magnificent: Eugen Sandow and the Beginnings of Bodybuilding*. Urbana and Chicago: University of Illinois Press, 1994.

Dickson, W. K.-L., and William Heise. "Sandow." Video by the Edison Manufacturing Co. 1894. Available online at https://www.loc.gov/item/00694298/.

Liederman, Earle. "My Muscles Keep Me Young—Says Sandow." Originally published in *Muscle Builder* (US), December 1924. Available online at http://physicalculturist.ca/sandow-muscles-keep-me-young/.

Liederman, Earle. "Sandow: My Impressions When We First Met." Originally published in *Muscle Power* (Canada), April/May 1946. Available online at http://www.davidgentle.com/sandow/liederman/sandow.html.

Mordden, Ethan. *Ziegfeld: The Man Who Invented Show Business*. New York: St. Martin's Press, 2008.

Pearl, Bill, George Coates, Tuesday Coates, and Richard Thornley Jr. *Legends of the Iron Game: Reflections on the History of Strength Training*. Vol. 1. Phoenix, OR: Bill Pearl Enterprises, 2010.

"Sandow as a Samson." *San Francisco Chronicle*, May 23, 1894, p. 13.

Sandow, Eugen, "My Reminiscences," *Strand Magazine*, February 1910, pp. 144–152. Available online at https://archive.org/stream/TheStrandMagazineAnIllustratedMonthly/TheStrandMagazine1910aVol.XxxixJan-jun#page/n161/mode/2up.

Sandow, Eugen. *Strength and How to Obtain It*. London: Gale & Polden, 1897. Available online at https://archive.org/details/strengthandhowt00sandgoog.

Sandow, Eugen, and G. Mercer Adam. *Sandow on Physical Training*. New York: J. Selwin Tait & Sons, 1894. Available online at https://archive.org/details/sandowgetsphysicl00sanduoft.

"Sandow in Court." *San Francisco Call*, April 21, 1894, p. 3.

Scott, Patrick. "Body-Building and Empire-Building: George Douglas Brown, the South African War, and *Sandow's Magazine of Physical Culture*." *Victorian Periodicals Review* 41, no. 1 (2008): pp. 78–94.

Waller, David. *The Perfect Man: The Muscular Life and Times of Eugen Sandow, Victorian Strongman*. Brighton, UK: Victorian Secrets, 2011.

Webster, David. *Barbells and Beefcake: Illustrated History of Bodybuilding*. Irvine, Scotland: David P. Webster, 1979.

For Brian, a.k.a. Coach Tate, and for B. J. and Drake

Acknowledgments

A special thank-you to the staff of the H. J. Lutcher Stark Center for Physical Culture and Sports at the University of Texas at Austin, where a large collection of Eugen Sandow materials is generously made available to the public. I was able to examine several bronze Sandow trophies, a painting of Sandow as a gladiator by E. Aubrey Hunt, volumes of Sandow's magazines, and more.

Quotation Sources

For more information about the sources below, please see the bibliography on page 39.

Page 3: "the Strongest Man on Earth": Waller, p. 91.

Page 7: "How is . . . Father?": Sandow, "My Reminiscences," p. 144.

Page 7: "The heroes . . . their bodies": Sandow, "My Reminiscences," p. 144.

Page 16: "Attend to . . . in the world": Ludwig Durlacher ("Professor Attila"), quoted in Waller, p. 23.

Page 24: "the Modern Hercules": "Sandow in Court."

Page 28: "The Event of the Century": "Sandow as a Samson."

Page 36: "the most perfect male specimen alive": Budd, p. 44.

Photo Credits

Page 36: Falk, Benjamin J., photographer. "[Eugene Sandow, Full-length Portrait, Standing, Leaning on Column, Facing Left, Wearing Wrestling Leotard, Roman Sandals, and Six-Pointed Star Pendant]." Photograph. Circa 1894. From Library of Congress: Lot 12388. https://lccn.loc.gov/91480334.
Page 38: Photo courtesy of Don Tate. Copyright © Jeffery Kieffer. All efforts have been made to obtain permission from the artist and copyright holder of the work. The publisher will be happy to correct any omission in future printings.

Published by Charlesbridge
85 Main Street
Watertown, MA 02472
(617) 926-0329
www.charlesbridge.com

Illustrations created digitally using Manga Studio
Display type set in Deco by Open Window
Text type set in Elmhurst by Christopher Slye
Color separations by Colourscan Print Co Pte Ltd, Singapore
Printed by 1010 Printing International Limited in Huizhou, Guangdong, China
Production supervision by Brian G. Walker
Designed by Diane M. Earley

Printed in China
(hc) 10 9 8 7 6 5 4 3 2 1

Library of Congress Cataloging-in-Publication Data
Names: Tate, Don, author.
Title: Strong as Sandow : how Eugen Sandow became the strongest man on earth / Don Tate.
Description: Watertown, MA : Charlesbridge, [2017]
Identifiers: LCCN 2016010219 (print)
   | LCCN 2016033884 (ebook)
   | ISBN 9781580896283 (reinforced for library use)
   | ISBN 9781607348863 (ebook)
   | ISBN 9781607348870 (ebook pdf)
Subjects: LCSH: Sandow, Eugen, 1867–1925. | Bodybuilders—United States—Biography. | Bodybuilding—History.
Classification: LCC GV545.52.S26 T37 2017 (print) | LCC GV545.52.S26 (ebook) | DDC 796.41092 [B]—dc23
LC record available at https://lccn.loc.gov/2016010219

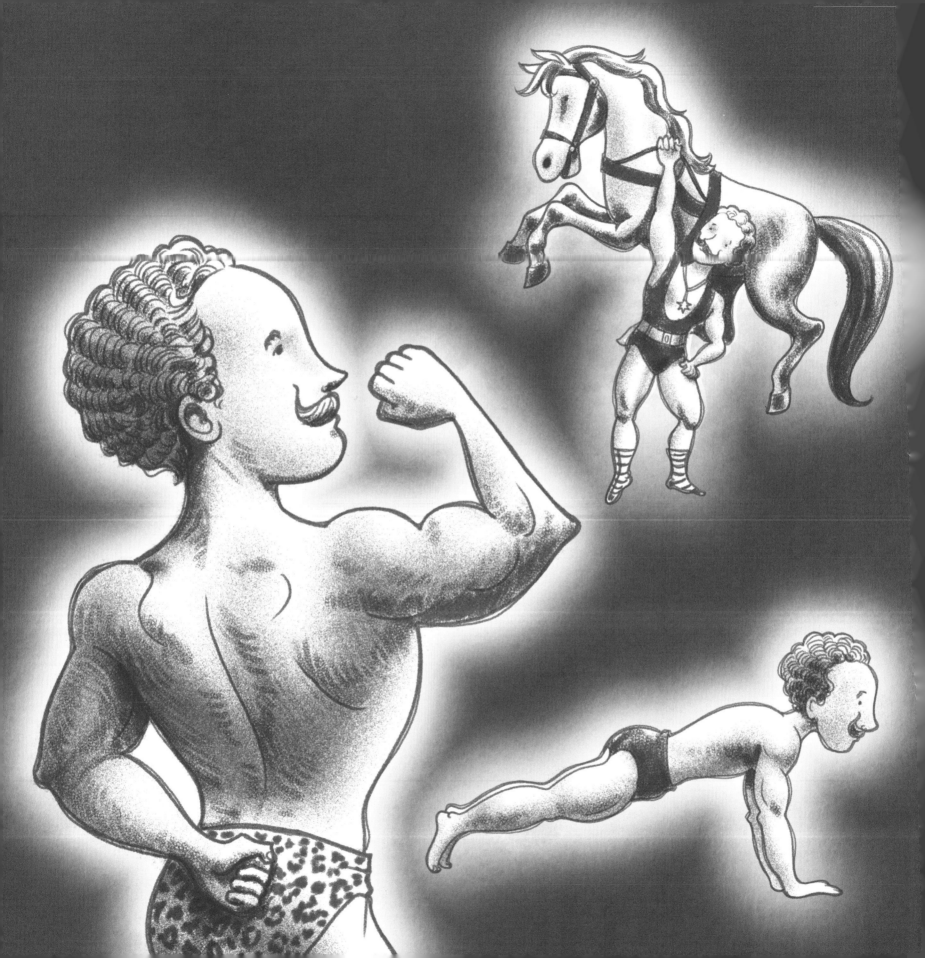